Absentminded PERFORMER

by Myka-Lynne Sokoloff
illustrated by Erin Eitter Kono

Harcourt
SCHOOL PUBLISHERS

Printed in China

ISBN 13: 978-0-15-350544-7
ISBN 10: 0-15-350544-3

Ordering Options
ISBN 13: 978-0-15-350335-1 (Grade 5 Below-Level Collection)
ISBN 10: 0-15-350335-1 (Grade 5 Below-Level Collection)
ISBN 13: 978-0-15-357542-6 (package of 5)
ISBN 10: 0-15-357542-5 (package of 5)

11 12 13 14 15   0940   12 11 10

My best friend, Julie, calls me "the absentminded perfessor." Of course, she means pro-fessor, but she says it the wrong way in jest. That means "in fun."

Julie calls me that since I always have my head in a book. I love reading all about inventions. I like inventing things, too. I don't really like getting up in front of others and speaking, though. Even though I like words, I can't always remember them. Sometimes the wrong words come out when I try to explain things. I am really kind of shy except with Julie.

One day my teacher announced that we were going to put on a class play. Mr. Greer always said that we should stretch ourselves. He meant we should try to do things that we didn't usually do. I guess that was why he asked me to take a leading role in the play.

Gulp. I groaned inside when he asked me. I did not want to disappoint him, so I agreed to take the part. Even before I knew anything about my part, I began to fret about learning the lines.

Mr. Greer told Julie she would be the stage manager. Her job was to make sure everything ran smoothly during the play. The only thing that made me feel better about getting up in front of a crowd was teasing Julie about being stage manager. Poor Julie was always disorganized. She lost stuff. She was all thumbs when it came to machines and fixing things.

Julie was not happy about her job for the play either. However, she liked to see the good side of things. "What's the worst that could happen?" she asked. "The curtain won't come down when it's supposed to?"

The play was about President Abe Lincoln
and the Civil War. I was Abe, so I had lots of lines,
including the Gettysburg Address. "Don't worry,"
Mr. Greer assured me. "I wouldn't have given you
the part if I didn't think you could handle it."

I was only four feet tall. The first thing I
would need to play Abe Lincoln was a good pair
of stilts. I poked around in my closet and found
some items that I could use to make a pair
of stilts.

I hoped the stilts would make me look more presidential. Then Mom helped make some pants that would cover them. I spent the next couple of weeks practicing with the stilts. Partly, I really wanted to get good at walking with them. Partly, I was avoiding learning my lines.

Finally, Julie sat me down. "It's time to learn your lines," she said. "I'll help you."

"Yeah. I'll help you be the stage manager," I said. "Why can't we just switch?"

"Mr. Greer says we have to stretch ourselves," she reminded me.

For the next two weeks, I tried to learn my lines. I read them to my family at dinner. I taped them to the mirror over the bathroom sink. Then I read them out loud when I brushed my teeth. I read them to the dog when I took her for a walk. Julie made me practice my lines at lunch and recess. Still, the words just wouldn't stay in my brain.

".. . government of the people, by the people, for the people, shall not perish from the earth."

government of the people by the people for the people shall not perish from the earth

Finally, Julie said, "You are so good at inventing things. Why don't you invent something that will help you with your lines if you get stuck?"

I decided to take Julie's advice. I poked around my room to find just what I needed. When I was done, just having my invention made me feel much better.

Still, on the day of the play, I was nervous. When the curtains opened, I was supposed to stride onto the stage and begin my first speech. My stilt feet felt glued to the floor. Mr. Greer nudged me. I stepped out onto the stage and cleared my throat.

9

As soon as I made my appearance, there was quite a ruckus. Everyone laughed at my outlandish costume. I was easily as tall as the real Abe Lincoln. I had a fake black beard glued to my chin.

The most important prop I had was my hat. I had written my lines on a strip of paper in teeny, tiny writing. After I wrote the lines, I wound the paper around two straws, like a scroll. I fixed the scroll to the brim of my hat so that I could turn it to see my lines. That way I didn't have to worry about forgetting my lines.

Everything was going pretty well. The other actors were doing a fine job. I knew most of my lines, and for those I didn't, my gadget worked like a charm. If I forgot what I was supposed to say, I casually looked up at the scroll for help. The other actors were pretty patient with me, and it actually enhanced my performance as I looked just like Abe Lincoln carefully choosing each word he would say next.

Then disaster struck. At the end of the second act, just as I had feared, the curtain was supposed to come down at a dramatic point—but, it didn't! I was all alone, stuck out there on stage. I had nothing to say and nowhere to go. The audience just stared at me and waited for something to happen.

It is altogether fitting and proper that we should do this

I knew I had to do something. I decided I would have to repeat the Gettysburg Address one more time. At least I had learned this part by heart.

Then I caught Julie's eye. She looked panicked as she tried to get the curtain to come down. I could see that the curtain was stuck above my head. I took my hat off and started swinging it over my head, with a grand gesture. "Four score . . ." *SWING* "and seven years ago, . . ." *SWING* "our forefathers . . . ," *SWING*.

"Four score . . .
and seven years ago, . . .
our forefathers . . . ,"

Since I was already so tall, I was able to smack the stuck part of the curtain with my hat. Right at the end of my Gettysburg Address speech, the curtain fell down, almost on top of me.

I looked over at Julie and gave her an OK sign. Then the other actors all filed out on stage and took a bow with me. Julie came out on stage and took a bow, too. The audience thought we were all great and clapped for a long time.

A little later, after I had changed out of my costume, I went back to the classroom. There I was greeted by the other kids who gave me a standing ovation.

Julie held her eyeglass case up to her mouth, like a microphone. "Ladies and gentlemen, may I introduce George Lu, the Absentminded Performer! He had big shoes (and a big hat) to fill, and he filled them beautifully," she proclaimed.

"With your help," I said. "Anyway, 'The world will little note nor long remember what we say here.'" I quoted Abraham Lincoln's words from the Gettysburg Address.

"Well said, George!" said Julie and Mr. Greer at the same time.

Think Critically

1. Who was telling the story?

2. Explain what Mr. Greer meant when he said that people should stretch themselves.

3. What was George's problem? How did he solve it?

4. How did George and Julie help each other?

5. Did anyone in the story remind you of someone you know?

 **Social Studies**

Lincoln Time Line The Gettysburg Address is a famous speech given by Abraham Lincoln in 1863. Find out some more about Abraham Lincoln. Then put together a time line of ten important events in his life.

School-Home Connection Share this story with someone at home. Discuss what you know about Abraham Lincoln and the Gettysburg Address.

Word Count: 1,178